MW01489207

GOOD CHRISTIAN GIRL

To anyone with a story similar to mine:

I see you. I am so sorry for any hurt you may still carry with you. Your experiences are valid, and how you choose to cope with them are also valid.

To anyone who has ever *caused* a story similar to mine:

Time's up.

Copyright © 2021 Holley Lunsford

All rights reserved.

Contents

INTRODUCTION

According to christianitytoday.com, which cites a study sponsored by LifeWay Christian Resources, "10 percent of Protestant churchgoers under 35 have left a church because they felt sexual misconduct was not taken seriously." According to Davidson College's Offices and Services webpage, as well as the webpages of several other colleges and universities that appear with a Google search for the definition of "sexual misconduct", sexual misconduct can best be described as "a broad range of behavior, from harassing statements to criminal sexual assault." In May of 2018, The Washington Post reported on a scandal that took place at Southeastern Baptist Theological Seminary in North Carolina in 2003 in which a woman who reported that she had been raped to the seminary's president Paige Patterson. Allegedly, Patterson encouraged the woman not to contact the police and then went on to

1

tell the woman that she needed to forgive the man who (again, allegedly) raped her.

These accusations against Paige Patterson were brought back to the surface after thousands of women had signed a petition in 2018 to have him removed as president of Southwestern Baptist Theological Seminary in Fort Worth, Texas. This petition came after recordings of Patterson encouraging an abused woman to pray for her husband rather than getting a divorce, as well as comments on a teen girl's body, were posted on a blog that garnered local attention.

According to NBC News, which cites an investigation conducted by The Houston Chronicle and San Antonio Express-News in 2019, "220 pastors, ministers, deacons, volunteers, Sunday school teachers, and others were found guilty of sexually abusing churchgoers" over the course of twenty years. According to that same investigation, "roughly 380 Southern Baptist church leaders and volunteers have faced allegations of sexual misconduct involving more than 700 victims". It seriously takes no effort to find pages upon pages of sexual misconduct that takes place in churches across the country, and that is just what is *actually* reported.

Stories like mine are nothing new. With the sweeping rise of the #MeToo movement, which "helps to improve awareness about sexual violence, showing just how widespread sexual harassment and assault really are" by encouraging people to open up about their experiences with sexual misconduct, people are finally starting to let their guards down and open up about their trauma in the name of justice and accountability.

This book is my story in my own words. For too long, the men surrounding me and "in charge" of me had complete control over the narrative of my sexual harassment. They silenced me with shame and weaponized Bible verses to protect their image. The trauma I experienced slowly made me realize that I wanted no part of an organization that silences their victims Some people assume that I am voicing my story as an act of anger or vengeance, and I can't say for sure that if I were on the outside looking in, I would think any differently. Frankly, I *have* spent a great deal of time being angry about what happened to me. I've also spent a great deal of time wanting some kind of punishment to rain down on the man who is responsible for having abused his position of authority over me in the church that I loved with my whole heart. I have also wanted some kind of comeuppance for the men who led that place, who supported *him* through that entire situation and turned their backs on me as though I didn't matter, or even exist. I will fully admit that in the past I have been guilty of wanting to somehow make them acknowledge their failure to minister to me, but I am beyond that now, I think. It's not about anger or vengeance anymore, not really.

The fact of the matter is that I share my story because what happened to me is simply unacceptable. What happened to me led to a plethora of personal struggles with my mental health that it took years to overcome. What happened to me changed the direction of my life; I can say in hindsight that it all worked out for the better, but in the midst of all of it, I was completely lost, drowning in loneliness and left without so much as a word of encouragement from the people who put me in that position in the first place.

I know that some people will hear my story and roll their eyes, muttering to themselves and to anyone who will listen that God doesn't want any perfect people, so who am *I* to judge my assailants? Some will hear my story and decide that it's not for them because it makes them too uncomfortable, and that is perfectly fair— what happened to me *should* make people uncomfortable. What should make people even *more* uncomfortable though, is the idea that my story could happen to someone else. Sadly, sexual harassment and assault does continue to happen in any and every setting. That's why I write and share my story: so those who will hear about my story will pay special attention to their church bodies, to their people, see when stories like mine are being swept under the rug, downplayed, or blown off completely and will speak up to make things right.

At the end of the day, if my story causes even one person to speak up and do what is *right*, it will all have been worth it.

CHAPTER ONE

At twenty-one years old, I was an English major in college. I had just gotten into my first serious relationship, which was in a "you can't tell anyone we're together yet" stage. I found out much later that the purpose of our relationship's secrecy provided him the opportunity to continue dating other girls. During this part of my life, I also worked as a nanny, a writing tutor at a local community college, and a kids' ministry worship leader and volunteer coordinator as well as an intern for my town's most popular church's worship band.

It was at That Church where I was sexually harassed by my "boss".

I use the term "boss" loosely because, to be honest, his position was a joke. He was more like the man that That Church had designated as my official babysitter. You might ask what exactly an internship for a modern, Baptist-ish non-denominational church in Texas requires. Good question! I did everything that the *actual* members of the worship band *didn't* want to do. I set up their music stands and microphones, I frequently cleaned out their refrigerator, I threw out all the trash they left out (which was pretty much everything, always), I picked up case after case of water and replenished their supply, I ordered and picked up their dinner on rehearsal nights, and on Sundays, I got up at 3 AM to pick up and deliver their breakfast then stayed at church until after 12 so I could also do my job in the kids' ministry. The dad of the two kids I nannied at the time called my internship "grunt work" jokingly, but he was right. That was exactly what my internship consisted of.

And all for what?

When I agreed to serve as the worship band's intern, I was told that the internship would be a preparatory stepping-stone to joining the worship band as an official member—a singer, and I *desperately* wanted that to happen. Since they were a large band, I would be put in the rotation as a singer if I joined the band , which meant that every few weeks or months, I would sing worship songs to the entire adult/family congregation and still be able to sing in kids' ministry every other week to much more dance-able songs. Back then, I considered it perfectly normal and healthy to spend more time in a church building sweating than at home doing things like homework, resting, or eating. As I devoted more and more time to the church, my self-care deteriorated.

One thing people told me with some frequency was the old cliché: "You can't pour from an empty cup." I knew this. But I didn't see any way to make my "cup" any less empty—I had to take a full load of college classes as an English major to make up for the full year I spent as a music major, earning virtually no usable credits toward my degree. I also *had* to work as much as I could so I could save up for a place of my own. I loved working in the kids' ministry because when I was there, I held a valid and valued role. It was the *only* area of my life at the time where I was not treated like a child or a servant of some kind, and at twenty-one years old, that was everything. Obviously, I couldn't give up my internship. Not when every week the church told me that they were just about ready to "move me" from intern to band member.

At the time, I was fully convinced that my responsibilities would magically decrease when they decided I was worthy to be an Official Member of the band. I believed, wholeheartedly, that the internship and all its associated duties would be passed on to someone else. Someone who would be lesser than me once I was in this fabulous, top-tier Church Clique. In hindsight, I see how naive I was to believe that. I remember one particular conversation with Andrew—the "boss" who supervised me for my internship—before things turned sour and made the truth so glaringly obvious.

Andrew was reclined with his feet up, phone in hand on the big couch backstage where the band relaxed before going onstage. From his seat, he watched me go back and forth to and from my car three times, carrying in the five cases of water I'd just bought the band. When he initiated the conversation that follows, he was watching me cut the cases of water open and stock the fridge with the water bottles.

"So let me ask you something, Holley," he began. I paused my work to look up at him expectantly. "How are you feeling in this internship?"

I remember that I paused to think before responding. The question itself was incredibly odd to me. I eventually replied: "Well, I like it! It's tough at times, but I look at it like I'm serving God by doing it. I *am* excited about getting to lead worship with y'all... Soon?" I put just enough of a question mark at the end of my sentence to remind him of his months-old agreement to move me into the rotation.

His face was blank except for the absentminded, wide-eyed expression that seemed to always be on it, but he nodded and said: "Oh yeah, we're excited to have you! I just wanna make sure, you know, that you're solid and ready, and that it won't put too much on your plate."

There it was: the truth. Of course, I didn't know it at the time. As I mentioned earlier, hindsight.

9

"Oh," I said, "no, don't worry about that! I *love* staying busy!"

I guess it didn't matter much how much I *loved* staying busy because that internship dragged on for months before they threw me anything even resembling an opportunity. Here was the new deal: I still had my internship, I still wasn't going to be singing with the Sunday morning band, but I *was* going to start singing back-up in the youth ministry band on Wednesday nights. Yay, me.

CHAPTER TWO

Months kept passing and my list of responsibilities didn't find any kind of relief. I would sleep *maybe* five hours a night if I was lucky, and I was spiraling into a mental and physical burnout that I willfully ignored, all with a smile on my face and a pep in my step. Because, that's what a Good Christian Girl does.

Before I go any further, let me give you a little background insight into the church where I spent the majority of my time for years and its basic philosophies. It's important that you understand the environment so that what happened to me and the events that followed make some kind of sense.

This church has pretty humble beginnings. It was founded by two brothers and the weekly services started in one of their living rooms. It got bigger and more popular and, naturally, branched out into a movie theater, a school cafeteria, and then eventually into an old grocery store. As it grew (and continues to grow), it became less like a church and more like a brand. I'm talking billboards, bumper stickers, clothing, and even a handful of catchy slogans that members can pull out of their pocket and throw at anyone who dares call them out or hold them accountable for anything. The slogans, in particular, put a bad taste in my mouth since they let people in That Church continue to do whatever they want to do— regardless of whom they hurt in the process—while still maintaining their righteous image.

Side note/word to the wise: if you're going to remind people that no one is perfect, then it *might* be a good idea to remember that very sentiment when you want to pass judgments on someone whose marriage failed or someone who relapsed into old habits, or... I don't know... a young, single, pretty woman who got sexually harassed by the leader of your curated clique, and who was only guilty of the heinous sin of being unmarried and pretty in the presence of a married man.

I digress.

This particular church prides itself on its ministry to men. Even I have to admit, it's a pretty smart way to go about it. My dad considers himself a Lutheran but I can still count on one hand the number of times he's attended a Sunday service in my life, so I can at least respect their approach to specifically get men to come to church. If the men are persuaded to attend, then it stands to reason that the families follow.

I do, however, believe the ministry to men focus leads to a whole lot of problems. Problems like hosting man-centric events every month where the topic of conversation seems to always be how it's impossible to *not* feel lustful when women do pretty much anything in the same space as them, like working out at the gym, or smiling at them in passing, or wearing their hair in a ponytail. At these events, the men are told things like they can't go more than three days without ejaculating and that masturbation *always* leads to addiction and to pornography. They are taught that they share responsibility for their lust and temptations with the women around them, whether those women know them or not and whether they even interact with them or not. In the simplest terms possible, the idea that men are the uncontrollable horn dogs who *will* take sex if it's available, regardless of who it is with, is widely perpetuated—at least enough for all the men I've talked to specifically about these monthly man-centric events to come away from the events with that idea burned into their minds.

As for the women, well, let's just say that we're taught different ideologies. For starters, in the years that I attended That Church, the subject of female lust came up only once, spoken of in an almost-whisper by the female speaker at the yearly women's conference in the type of tone that suggested that it was about as real as Santa Claus and only being brought up for the sake of the naive few that still believed it existed.

"I mean, sure, of *course,* we struggle with lust too, it's just *different!*"

What was emphasized for women was the Bible verse commanding wives to submit to their husbands. Now, I will go on record and say that I am no theologian. I did not go to seminary school even for a semester. But I *am* a researcher. An avid one. I guess it's the English major/future librarian in me. I've also read the Bible in its entirety multiple times, and as someone who has read the Bible multiple times *and* done extensive research looking into this very topic if only for the sake of finding how my love of God and my feminist ideals can co-exist (spoiler alert: it's not hard for those ideas to do so) I feel pretty confident in the analysis of that verse that says wives need to not go out of their way to openly oppose their husbands. It doesn't mean to be a doormat for their husbands.

That's not exactly how this man's man church sees that verse. Surprise, surprise. No, the Powers That Be in That Church tend to take that verse to mean that women are indeed the weaker sex (which doesn't seem to add up too well with the idea that we're meant to control not only our female lusts, but the lusts of every man we come across as well—go figure) and we need to follow our man's

14

lead in all things and please him no matter what. On Mother's Day one year, the head pastor's wife even taught a whole sermon on how "submission is a woman's strength!" Happy Mother's Day, I guess?

So that's the very basics of what women are taught there. We shouldn't be the heads of our families (special circumstances like widowhood aside) but we do bear the burden of making sure that men aren't tempted by us because, naturally, that would lead to pornography addiction. We're also encouraged to be forgiving if our husbands do fall weak to temptation and end up cheating on us in any capacity. But also, we should help them *not* be tempted by anyone outside of our marriages by making ourselves pleasing to them. Oh, and by making them ejaculate at *least* every three days. Single women need to learn and eternalize all of these lessons to prepare themselves for their future husbands, which after all, is the prize for the well-behaved Good Christian Girl.

Even when I was amid this mentality and lifestyle, surrounded by all of these so-called truths, I'll admit that I only bought into some of it. As I said, I hold very feminist ideals and I certainly had the foundation for them back then, even if they weren't yet fully developed. For one thing, I don't think I ever bought into the idea that men are just naturally uncontrollable horn-dogs without being taught that they are. I've also always held the belief that people, regardless of their sex or gender, are fully responsible for

15

their actions. However, I was wise enough even then to keep such radical ideas to myself.

I did have the rather rare privilege of being in a leadership role; I was in charge of worship and the volunteer worship team (consisting of singers and dancers) in kids' ministry. After a while, I was also even allowed to teach the kids' ministry sermon on occasion. Don't fool yourself, like I did, into thinking that they were being in any way progressive by giving me that position. John, the head of all kids' ministry at the time, offered me that position and was free to do so because kids' ministry was left to its own devices. Plus, and let's just be honest here, while kids' ministry introduces kids to Biblical principles, it is also a kind of Sunday morning childcare, and childcare is still very much viewed as women's work. As long as I didn't draw too much attention to myself (*that* would be vain and not at all Christ-centered), I doubt that The Powers That Be would've ever encouraged me to step down from that position.

CHAPTER THREE

While I was That Church's do-everything girl, I only had classes on Tuesdays and Thursdays at my college, which helped me work as many jobs as I did. Mondays were particularly hectic. I'd work in the writing lab as a tutor from the morning until mid-afternoon when I'd leave to go pick up the kids I nannied from their bus stop, take them home and be with them until one of their parents came home in the early evening. Then I'd head to That Church to start setting up for the worship band's practice until it was time to go get the band's dinner, at which point I'd leave and grab it from wherever it had been ordered from. Then I'd come back and set it all out for them, and do whatever else needed to be done for them before practice started. Then I'd head home to do all of the homework and class readings I'd need to have done by morning.

One particular Monday evening sometime in October sticks out to me more than others in my memory. It'll become pretty

17

obvious why soon enough. I was setting out the band's dinner and chatting with Andrew, who had just gotten a bad weave and was trying to hide the roots of it under a hat. Every year, he played Jesus in a musical production of the entire life of Christ that was put on in a neighboring town. It's incredibly popular if you're from the area. This particular evening, as I set out the band's dinner and he stood there with a small cup of coffee in his hand, I couldn't help noticing that he didn't reach around me to grab his dinner before I was finished arranging food and plates like he usually did.

"Are you not eating?" I asked.

"Oh, no," he replied, "I'm going to a concert tonight with a friend and we'll be grabbing dinner on the way."

"Oh, cool! Who are you going to see?" I asked. I was genuinely curious. What kind of music does a worship leader, would-be Julliard attendee who played Jesus Christ in an annual show for goodness' sake even listen to?

Coheed and Cambria. Admittedly pretty cool.

That night, long after my parents and sister had gone to sleep (I forget the exact time, but it would have been after midnight at least), I was awake and upstairs in my family's computer room. I was going back and forth between Spanish homework and checking Facebook. I was still relatively new to social media; my mom didn't allow me to have a MySpace until my junior year of high school, and

18

the only reason she gave me the go-ahead to have a Facebook the year after that was because almost every college scholarship I was applying for had their application on their Facebook page. On this particular night, Facebook was still what I was most active on. I vaguely knew about Instagram, but it seemed too confusing to me at the time to bother with setting one up for myself. So, when I say that I was sheltered, I mean that I was *SHELTERED*. In fact, I'd just gotten my first smartphone a few months before.

At one of these ridiculous early-morning hours, I got a text. From none other than the bad-weave- boss himself, Andrew.

It wasn't too unusual to get a text from him between the days when I completed my internship duties. If there was extra work around That Church that needed to be done, or if I'd forgotten something that I was supposed to do or pick up for them, he'd text me to let me know what needed to get done. In all honesty, I didn't think anything of it when I saw that he'd texted that night.

Andrew: Hey Holley, you up?

Me: Yep, doing homework. Everything all right?

Andrew: Oh yeah, it's awesome

Do you have Snap?

Me: Sorry, I don't know what that is

Andrew: Snapchat

If you don't have it, you should get it, we can talk on there

Me: It's an app?

Andrew: Lol yeah

I know what you're thinking, I know. Huge red flag. But I genuinely knew *nothing* about Snapchat back then. If I had, I would have seen this conversation for what it was and disengaged entirely. The truth is that while it *did* annoy me that he couldn't just say what he needed to say in the medium he was *already* speaking to me in, he was my boss. To this day, even after years of forcing myself to learn to establish healthy boundaries with people, I still find that I'm terrified of telling any authority figure "no", of calling them out on their bullshit, and of asking them questions that could help me do a better job if answered but would make me look stupid if asked. Even though my internship was unpaid, the fact that Andrew could put me on stage with the worship band on Sundays made him an authority figure that I especially felt compelled to not piss off with things like boundaries and, in hindsight, I think he must have figured that out pretty quickly.

So, I downloaded Snapchat and tried to figure out how exactly it worked while simultaneously letting my boss know that we could now speak the way he so clearly felt compelled to, so I could finish my Spanish and get at least three hours of sleep for school.

The conversation was odd, but innocent at first. I complained about how nothing I was looking at on the app made any sense to me. Texting, I understood. You compose a message, type it, send it, and receive a reply. The icons all made sense. It was simple and straightforward. Snapchat had its main page as just your camera? How are you supposed to effectively communicate using only pictures? Could you add text? It *had* to let you do that, right?

Andrew kept "lol" -ing and told me how to add text to pictures. We were using the message function that didn't require pictures at all, which made me even more confused as to why he'd wanted to talk to me on here in the first place, but I still didn't spot the giant red flag waving in my face because A) I'm a moron—a naive, too-trusting one at that, and B) Andrew is… I'll just say it, he's a weird fucking dude. I mean, the whole reason he got the "Jesus weave" glued to his scalp in all its dirty, uneven glory was that he thought putting on the wig he used to wear instead was too much of

21

a hassle. So, I didn't call him out on the bullshit I *did* see that he was pulling (texting me past midnight, asking me to download a whole new app that I didn't understand, and then *still* not telling me why he texted in the first place) but I *did* decide to try and cut to the chase. Not outright, of course, but in a Good Christian Girl sort of way.

Me: Oh, I almost forgot! Did you need me to help with something at church this week? Is that why you texted?

Andrew: Nah, it's all good

Me: Oh, okay. Well, thanks for teaching me about Snapchat! I guess I'll see you Sunday :)

Andrew: I was looking through your pictures on Facebook. You are gorgeous.

I'll admit, that one made me feel as though my stomach had dropped right to the floor while my heartfelt as though it leaped to my throat and was trying to be vomited out.

When Andrew first came to That Church and joined the worship band, I did have a bit of a crush on him. It was to be expected, I guess. He was single at the time, new in town, passionate about music, and a Christian. At least, that's what I'd heard about him in the church social circles I was in. The crush I'd had on him was a lot like a celebrity crush in that all you know about the person is what you've heard *about* them since they're too far out of your reach for you to ever learn anything by actually talking to them. For a hot minute, my mom was convinced that he also had a crush on me because it looked a lot like he kept looking (ahem, *staring*) at me on Sundays while he was onstage playing.

The seats in church sort of wrapped around the stage, and if you were to stand on the stage and face the far wall, my mom, sister, and I would be on your left, three rows from the front, *always*. It wasn't as though he ever faced our direction naturally while he was onstage; he (and everyone else) was pointed towards the middle, where the bulk of the people sat. Yet for some reason, Andrew would always turn his head in my direction for an extended period, making eye contact with me even. It was the closest thing to being noticed by an *actual* celebrity that I'd ever experienced. I screamed when he added me on Facebook.

But then he started dating Kelly, a girl who had been in the grade above me in high school, and they quickly got engaged. Then married. Then they had their first baby. I was genuinely happy for them, though. My mom and I had even made them a baby blanket. To be honest, it didn't take too long after being Andrew's Facebook friend for my crush on him to fizzle out. Not only did I get my first glimpse at the fact that (as I've said) he's a weird fucking dude, but I also saw that up close he's just not all that cute to me.

When someone is elevated on a stage that's five feet tall with a guitar in their hands and a microphone in front of their face with a spotlight shining down on them, it's surprisingly easy to believe they're some sort of discount Gavin Degraw. Take all that away, and you come to realize that your idols are just as human as you are, and just as capable of having acne or beady eyes or buck teeth. Needless to say, the shallow crush left just as quickly as it had come, and I was glad for him and the family he created for himself, even before I ever really got to know him.

So, when he said I was gorgeous, I *finally* started to feel as uncomfortable as I already should have felt. But I didn't want to piss him off, so I tried to be the polite, Good Christian Girl, as always.

> Me: Oh, thanks... I think Kelly is so gorgeous, you're so lucky!

Andrew: I love the one of you in your Star Trek dress

> Me: Oh, you like Star Trek?

Andrew: You looked so sexy!

I remembered the picture he was referring to. Months before, I'd attended a Star Trek convention dressed as a female Vulcan in a classic Star Trek blue uniform dress. The dress itself was high-collared, long-sleeved, and since I'd lost a significant amount of weight between the day I bought it and the day I wore it, it had fit somewhat loosely around my midsection. But it did end about four or so inches above my knees. Before the convention, I'd taken a picture of my outfit and shared it on Facebook with my head cropped out since I hadn't put on my wig or Vulcan makeup.

I was proud of that picture. I've struggled with weight and with hating my body for my whole life… I still do. That picture showed what years of effort had done, and it made me feel good.

But then Andrew, my married boss with a shitty, ratty weave glued to his head said that to me. Suddenly, knowing that he looked at that picture, which didn't even include my friggin' head, I felt ashamed. Dirty. I didn't even know how a polite, Good Christian Girl would respond to both *not* piss off her boss while still expressing the very icky feeling she was currently having *because* of said boss. So, I didn't respond at all. That didn't stop him, though.

Andrew: I want to see more of that little body

Andrew: You can send pictures on here and they'll get deleted automatically

Andrew: You're just so sexy!

I saw that he was still typing. I felt my face flush and begin to tingle like a limb that's fallen asleep. My heart was beating hard enough that I felt it on every inch of my body and heard it in my ears, along with a high-pitched ringing. I felt as though I couldn't breathe. I used to have panic attacks in high school, but I hadn't had one in at least three years by this point, so it took me a moment to recognize that that's what was happening to me. I needed to make him stop.

Me: Oh wow, it's late

That seemed to do the trick. I waited a minute or so and got no response. I shut down the family computer and went to bed, shaking. I didn't even finish my homework.

CHAPTER FOUR

The day after my Snap-exchange with Andrew, I went about my day at school feeling like I'd swallowed a rock. I was nervous and ashamed in a way I had never felt. Of what, exactly, I still don't know completely. I kept running through every single interaction I'd ever had with Andrew before that night. What did I do, what was the *exact* moment when I did whatever it was I did to make him think that I was the type of girl who wanted to sext with a married man? In my opinion, if I had engaged in what he'd been trying to start, he would have been cheating on Kelly—the mother of his child—and I would have been the Other Woman he cheated on her with. I wanted to know exactly what I did to make him believe I wanted that.

I could think of nothing except maybe that I tried too hard to be pretty when I was at church (which was always). No matter how much manual labor I knew I'd have to do, I always wore mascara to make my eyes pop. My hair was always flat-ironed and combed smooth. I always made sure to wear flattering jeans with flowery, flowy chiffon tops over solid and modest camisoles, like a Good Christian Girl. The fact of the matter is that I always wanted to look my best because it made me feel good to do so, and *that* was the only thing I could think of that caused Andrew to talk to me the way he did. I felt like a whore.

And what about Andrew? Before this, in my mind, he was weird, yes, but also goofy, artistic, and overall harmless. I saw him as an excellent example of using your God-given talents *for* God. I saw him as someone who was so on fire for God that he worked as hard as anyone has ever worked to be a good person in every way— n example for others to follow. The idea that it was him, of all people, who made me feel so slimy and violated caused cognitive dissonance in me that I don't think anything could have prepared me for. I simply couldn't sit with it.

At this point, I hadn't told anyone about the conversation because honestly, I wanted to forget about it. Better yet, I wanted it to have never happened at all. Then, in my last (and favorite) class of the day, I got a text. From Andrew. Seeing his name gave me a sudden urge to vomit. But I opened it anyway.

Andrew: Hey Holley! Sorry to bother you, but my phone got hacked last night. Still not sure how lol but I wanted to give you a heads up in case you were wondering :)

I let out a sigh of relief and instantly felt the knots in my belly loosen at last. Desperate as I was to release myself of the dissonance and horrible feelings that had filled me all day long, I didn't even allow myself to acknowledge all of the obvious questions that arose from his explanation, all the holes that one wouldn't even have to try very hard to poke in his very, very, very obvious lie. I refused to *not* believe it because I *needed* it to be true.

So, I did believe it. I believed it when I told my mom about the whole silly thing when I got home from classes. I laughed at how foolish I had been to worry. *Obviously*, that hadn't been Andrew. I think that my mom also wanted to believe the lie because she didn't say anything to match the skepticism playing out on her face. I believed his phone was hacked when I left my house to pick up my nanny-kids from the bus stop and take them home. Hell, I even believed it while I was at that job preparing their dinner and got a call from the church office. Despite my persistence to believe the lie he had fed to me, that number still made my heart drop.

"Hello?" I answered.

"Hey, Holley! It's J.T. Glover from the church, how are you?"

J.T. was another pastor at That Church, though he rarely preached on Sundays. I'm sure he was in charge of *something* in That Church, but for the life of me, I could not tell you what exactly that was. I still can't. I saw him often since I was there all the time, but the only thing I knew about him was that besides his friendliness and constantly cheerful demeanor, he was pretty unremarkable compared to everyone else on staff. Sorry. Now that I think about it, though... Given some of the other members of that staff, being a bit unremarkable is a good thing. All the "remarkable" people in That Church tend to develop the arrogance that allows them to feel good about taking advantage of other people. I suppose when you have countless people surrounding you, telling you daily how incredible you are and what a great, shining example you are to the church body, arrogance is inevitable.

Anyway.

"Oh, I'm good, J.T... How about you?"

"Awesome, awesome, hey I don't know what your schedule looks like with school and everything, but do you think you could come by the church offices tomorrow morning for a quick meeting?"

I swallowed down the lump that had already formed in my throat and said "Sure, I could be there. Say, 10?" Even though I was determined to believe that I had been subject to a phone hacker's amusement, I couldn't trick myself into believing that this meeting was unrelated. I felt so sure that I was going to be in trouble, and the

idea alone made it damn near impossible to get through the rest of

that day with any measure of peace.

CHAPTER FIVE

I got to the church at 9:45 am. My hair was still wet from the shower I had rushed through. I sat in the waiting area, fidgeting restlessly with my phone. Before I'd left the house, my parents told me to let them know how the meeting went. My mom suggested that maybe they'd decided to put me in the band, but I don't think either one of us believed that, even a little.

At 10:05 am I was still waiting when Andrew walked in. He flopped down on the couch opposite the one I was sitting on. I remember that he was wearing a fedora to hide the shoddy weave that dangled, still dirty, still *clearly* not brushed, around his face. He sat reclined into the couch, one ankle resting casually on the opposite leg's knee, and tried making lighthearted small talk with me. After all, it was just the two of us there, and he needed someone to enjoy that fabulous hat. I humored him by asking about the concert, but I could barely force myself to look at him.

Finally, J.T. came through the door that led into the offices and smiled, saying: "Oh good, you're *both* here! Come on back!"

Andrew and I both hopped up at the same time, but I let him go first to follow J.T. as he led us through the maze of halls and rooms to his office. Already I felt like I was going to cry.

When we got to J.T.'s office, I was invited to sit on a faux leather futon while the two men sat in chairs on the other side of the small room. J.T. began by leading us in a brief prayer before we started, asking God to give all of us some of His grace and wisdom, and His forgiving heart. When I managed to choke out an "Amen", it was barely a whisper. With a prayer *that* specific, I knew that whatever came from this meeting would not be good for me.

When I looked up, I noticed that Andrew was still bent forward, forearms on his knees and hands still firmly clasped in Prayer Mode, and his face was still pointed towards the floor. The ratty weave formed a curtain on either side of his face. Gone was the man who flopped onto the couch like he was in his own house making small talk with me. It was like he was putting on a show of humility.. He acted as though by saying the prayer, J.T. had shouted "ACTION!" and now he was giving a performance. I remember thinking, even while I had to remind myself to breathe in and out, that it was like a switch was flipped inside his head. I found that incredibly unsettling.

33

J.T. addressed me: "Well Holley, we appreciate you taking the time to come to this meeting today. I want to start by saying that you're not in trouble, so please don't think that. You know we all have our sin and just junk that we have to fight against, and I know people sometimes think that being a pastor or even," he gestured towards Andrew, "a worship leader who also plays Jesus every year means that we don't have to struggle much, but that is simply not true. I have my sin, Andrew has his sin, and we've got to work diligently to fight against our temptations. Sometimes we fail."

I nodded. My heart was pounding in my ears and I felt heat rising from my chest to my cheeks, but I said nothing. Andrew still hadn't looked up. *What is this about?* Please *just get on with it,* I thought.

J.T. continued: "Part of what we're called to do is be there to help one another out through all those times we fail... To forgive, just like we've been forgiven. But that can only happen when we seek forgiveness through confession, and I'm going to let Andrew do that right now."

At last, I saw Andrew's face not the top of a fedora as he looked up towards me. Now his expression was solemn compared to the absentminded expression he typical wore.

"Holley," he started hesitantly, "I don't even know where to start. I went out the other night and drank. I got drunk and was just in an extremely dark place. I know that I talked to you through Snapchat… I don't know what I said, but I know it was inappropriate. I not only disrespected my wife, but I disrespected you as well, and I am so sorry. I pray that you can forgive me."

I blinked at the two of them a few times as they looked at me expectantly. Finally, I said the only phrase that kept being screamed in my head: "I'm confused." I took a few breaths, unsure of where to go from there at first. I looked at Andrew. "When you texted me to say that your phone got hacked… You li—that was a lie?"

They both nodded, Andrew looking at me, J.T. looking at Andrew.

"It was," Andrew said, "and I could not be more sorry."

Again, they both looked at me as though they expected me to respond. The problem was that I had no idea what to say. What could I say?

"Did I—" I practically stuttered, "did I do something to… Was there something I did to cause… To make this happen?"

They both began shaking their heads before I could even spit out my question, and J.T. assured me: "Not at all! This is on Andrew, 100%. He knows it, I know it, Kelly knows it, you did nothing wrong. No one blames you at all."

I took a shaky breath of relief. Though I didn't ask specifically about Andrew's wife, I was glad to have the reassurance that she didn't hate me.

Andrew went back to looking forlorn and J.T. cleared his throat awkwardly. I looked at him.

"Holley, I have to ask, are you still dating Cameron?" He asked in a quiet, almost nervous voice.

Cameron was, at the time, one of the volunteers for the Sunday technology team. He was also in my Bible study group. We hung around one another while at church and even had a bit of a flirtationship for all of five minutes, but we were ultimately just friends. I liked Cameron because we listened to the same music, and he was basically covered in tattoos. Even if I had been seriously interested in dating him, it would have never worked out. The tattoo thing was a major no-no for my "Lutheran" dad, and— if I'm being totally honest—Cameron just wasn't very smart. All my jokes seemed to fly over his head and that is, was, and always will be a *major* turn-off. Still, we got along really well, and I enjoyed hanging around the church and Bible study with him. He was just easy to be around. But *dating*? No. Hell no. So J.T.'s question threw me more than a little off.

"Um, no?" I said, "We've never dated."

He nodded a little. I think he was surprised. "Oh, okay," he said, "well then we won't need to call him in for a meeting."

Later, after the shock wore off, it would strike me as quite odd that J.T. seemed more nervous about the idea of Andrew having to have this talk with Cameron, whom he'd assumed was the man in my life. It still strikes me as odd to this day. At that very moment, though, I had a much more important issue on my mind:

"My internship—" I blurted out, surprising even Andrew enough that he looked back up at me without even a hint of that humbled sadness on his face. I collected myself and tried again: "I mean... I'm still the worship intern, right? Until I can join the band?"

J.T.'s face became stone. I guess the penny they'd been waiting for me to hear finally dropped.

"Well," he said with a glance at Andrew, "it would probably be best for everyone if you stepped down from that for now. No one thinks it was your fault but y'all being around each other right now... It would probably just place an unnecessary strain on Andrew and Kelly's marriage, and of course, we don't want to make *you* uncomfortable, Holley."

There it was. The reason this whole thing had to be a face-to-face meeting instead of an email or, say, a phone call that could have been recorded. I was getting fired from my unpaid internship because of this. How could they look me in the face and say it wasn't

37

my fault when clearly it was? It *had* to have been. People don't get fired from things for stuff that isn't their fault.

I felt the blood drain from my face and the inside of my chest turned ice cold. I would never get to sing with the band on Sunday mornings. They might as well have kicked me out of the church altogether.

I nodded, said I understood and left.

CHAPTER SIX

I managed to hold it together until I called my mom from the church parking lot to tell her what happened. Through my sobs, I heard her tell me to meet her where she worked, so I did. Once there, I relayed my entire conversation with Andrew and J.T., but I guess she needed to hear it straight from the horse's mouth because she called the church office then and there to ask J.T. for a meeting of her own. At *that* meeting, he told both of my parents more or less the same things he'd told me, only without Andrew present. He did tell them he was sorry it had happened though, so I guess that's something.

Meanwhile, I guess word had spread within the church offices because I got a text from Brook, aka Mrs. That Church herself. Brook was married to Aaron, who was pastor over the worship team (so Andrew's boss as well as the whole band's boss, I suppose). Brook was also pretty much the star of the worship band, so she was kind of my idol. For her part, I think she saw herself as something of a mentor to me.

In her text, she asked only if I wanted to come over to her house, and at that moment, I could think of nowhere else I would have rather been.

When I pulled into their driveway, Aaron was outside cleaning his truck. He didn't say anything to me, in fact, I don't think he so much as *looked* at me, but he did tell his two small sons to stay outside with him while I went into the house to see Brook.

I once again broke down in tears while I told her everything. She let me talk while she just nodded at all the appropriate times, but it was clear that I wasn't telling her anything she didn't already know. When I told her how guilty I felt, how this whole thing *had* to be my fault, she encouraged me to "take those thoughts captive" so that "Satan doesn't get a foothold". She said other things too, I guess, to make me feel better, but it kept coming back to that. Take my thoughts captive.

After I calmed down and fresh tears were no longer worming their way out of my eyes, I confessed to her how embarrassed I was by this whole situation. It was true that I felt dirty because Andrew had outright asked to see my body—a body that I desperately wanted to be proud of—and not only did Kelly know about it, but so did the entire pastoral staff at That Church, which consisted of no fewer than six men. What was worse was that it was clear that they had *all* learned about this situation before anyone had decided to even include me in the conversation. It was humiliating. I tried communicating all of this to Brook at her house, on her screened-in back porch where we sat, but to this day I'm not sure she understood. She was in the central "clique" of That Church, and I was still very much an outsider who didn't even get a say in the narrative that was being spread about me.

The most compelling evidence I have that she didn't understand what I was feeling is the fact that she responded to my confession with: "Well Biblically, Kelly has the right to divorce after this, but I think instead she is committed to trying to heal their marriage."

Yeah… Thanks, I guess?

When I left, I proceeded through the rest of my day with business as usual, but I had what felt like a ten-pound weight on my chest. I was heartbroken. Losing the grunt work aspect of my internship wasn't so bad, but in the time I'd spent doing it, I felt like I had gotten close with all the members of the worship band. They were more than idols to me now; I felt accepted and liked by them. Aside from the fact that I cleaned up before and after them and got their meals and the fact that *those* were the only times some of them even spoke to me, I felt like they were my friends. I mourned the loss of that time with them.

I also mourned the loss of all my time at That Church. When you're any place as often as I was there, it's bound to start feeling like a second home: familiar. And comforting. And it seemed to me as though I'd arrived "home" to find that the family changed the locks while I was away.

Above all, I mourned that I'd never be asked to join the Sunday worship band. This alone shattered me. Ever since I joined That Church, I had dreamt of singing on Sunday mornings about how strong Christ's love is. I wanted so badly to be on that stage singing to the God I loved with like-minded people around me, my hands raised far above my head, my eyes closed, my voice forming a tether connecting me to the Creator of the Universe, and Him smiling down on me, whispering in a voice only I would be able to hear: "you make Me so proud".

And now I knew that I would never get to have that moment.

CHAPTER SEVEN

About a week or so passed before I got a call from Aaron, Brook's husband. I almost didn't answer the phone but changed my mind right before it went to voicemail.

One of the first things he gave me was an apology.

"Holley, I want you to know how sorry I am about how all this has been handled."

"No, I understand—"

"No seriously! After you came over that day, I brought it up at the weekly pastor meeting. I told 'em: 'Andrew is the one who did wrong, why are we punishing Holley for it?' and everyone agreed. So, if you want to come back into your internship role, and I completely understand if you don't, it is yours again and I'll be the one kind of over you."

"Yes, yes, of course!" I said, feeling warmth suddenly enter my body again.

Aaron asked me what exactly all of my responsibilities were. I filled him in on all of the duties I had to perform weekly for them, and even he seemed a little surprised at everything. He said that *he* would take care of some of the heavy lifting (like the literal heavy lifting) but then gave me some newer, more clerical responsibilities like printing and making copies of each week's setlists, lyrics, and chord progressions.

Another new development in my internship: payment.

"It's not much, I'm not gonna lie. But for as much as you do for us, you need to be on the payroll. So it'll be $150 a month. Sound good?"

It was everything.

In addition to all of this overwhelmingly exciting news, Aaron also told me that it had been decided that Andrew would go on a six-week unpaid leave. It was expected that during those six weeks, he and Kelly would participate in the once per week marriage ministry. He let me know, even though I didn't ask, that they were going to work through it together.

He also informed me that, during the sermon that coming Sunday, the head pastor would share with the whole church body the reason they wouldn't be seeing Andrew onstage for a while. He assured me that my name and the details would be left out of the announcement, though. *Okay,* I thought, *whatever.*

I never did hear that announcement, because I spent that whole Sunday morning in kids' ministry finding ways to keep busy. My mom heard it, though, and said it was fine. No real details, just vague statements about sin and falling short and needing to get realigned with God. *Okay,* I thought, *whatever.*

CHAPTER EIGHT

The next six weeks, while Andrew was gone, were great. I was finally getting paid *something* for all the time I was spending at That Church. Kids' ministry was great too, and I was still in the worship band for the youth ministry on Wednesday nights as a backup singer. As a boss, Aaron was great. He answered every question I ever had for him with straightforwardness—yes, no, *this* is how you should do x,y,z, *this* is why we do it this way… You get the point. He never texted me anything last-minute or after hours, and he kept things professional at all times. I appreciated that. I still do. I still wasn't getting asked to join the Sunday worship band, but it felt like it was only a matter of time. On Sundays, when he wasn't on the main stage, Aaron would pop into kids' ministry from time to time while I was leading worship there.

One Sunday in particular, I was just getting the kids started with my favorite worship song of all time: "Like A Lion" by Newsboys.

That song lit a fire in me regularly, but when I saw Aaron stick his head into the kids' ministry area, I put my *back* into it. He stayed for the whole song. As I watched him casually stroll out of the room from my spot on *my* stage, trying to catch my breath, I felt certain that he'd seen just how much I could offer to the band; more than just my talent but my *fire* too. Still, the invitation never came my way. *Soon,* I kept telling myself.

Then the six weeks came to an end. I knew Andrew would be back onstage six days ahead of time because I showed up for my duties on the band's practice night with their dinner, and there he was backstage. I asked Aaron who was in charge of me now, and he said that Andrew would be resuming *all* of his old responsibilities, including me.

I was sad that Aaron couldn't still be in charge of me. He made me feel comfortable in a way that I knew I could never feel around Andrew again. I never felt looked down upon by Aaron or objectified in any way. He treated me like someone who worked for him but was worthy of every respect that anyone else was worthy of. More than that, he had been the only person in the whole church that tried to do the right thing and who stood up for me through the whole Andrew thing. I never thanked him for that simple kindness, but I hope he knows somehow how much that still means to me, even if we haven't talked in years.

47

I don't know what I had expected for Andrew's first Sunday morning back if anything. I guess I assumed that Andrew would be back, everyone would notice, but no one would say anything and just act as though he had never left. So, when I sat beside my mom, sneaking in after the service had already started as always, I was honestly baffled by the smoke coming out of her ears and the fire she was breathing.

Yes, I am exaggerating about the smoke and fire, but you get the idea. She wasn't even listening to the sermon, just staring down at her sermon notes while she doodled on them the whole time.

"Well. He's back," she stated flatly at the end. "Did you know about the little *speech* they let him give?"

I hadn't known. I still don't know what exactly was said and I kind of don't want to know, even now. It just would have been nice to have been able to warn my mom about it ahead of time, like I had when he was making his exit.

CHAPTER NINE

For a few months, I kept going about all my internship business, ignoring how uncomfortable I felt having to answer to Andrew again. At least now he didn't text me outside of internship hours. For his part, Andrew made it his business to be *extra* formal anytime I was near. Like, if I was standing at the table setting up a buffet-style spread for the band and he had to walk past me, he practically scaled the wall on the opposite side of the room to get around me. It was like I existed inside a radioactive bubble.

I also noticed that the entire band would now get quiet whenever I got near if Andrew was with them. *That* made me feel like I was in a Christian reboot of Mean Girls.

On one occasion, I arrived at That Church early for my internship duties just so I could talk with Andrew and clear the air. He welcomed me into his office (making a point to open the door as wide as it would go) and invited me to sit in the chair right in front of his desk while he remained standing behind his desk. I told him that I wanted us to be cool with one another. If he believed that I wasn't at fault for what happened, then I didn't understand why being there and doing my job had to feel so awkward and gross. He apologized and, to his credit, admitted that he was just uncomfortable and didn't know when he wouldn't be.

On another occasion, I arrived early to discuss when I might be able to join the band on Sundays... You know, the whole reason I was doing that internship in the first place. It had been over a year at this point since I'd started and was told that it was only temporary, and I just wanted a time frame so I didn't have to keep torturing myself with wondering when, when, *when*?

At first, Andrew acted surprised, saying: "Oh we all just thought you wanted to just stick with kids' ministry, that you had found your niche there!" I pointed out that, while it was true that I *did* love doing kids' ministry, I had always maintained that what I wanted to do was "grown-up" worship on Sundays, at least once every couple of months. I said that I really could not imagine how "they" had gotten any other impression. Even John, my boss in kids' ministry, knew that I'd jump at the chance to do anything with the main worship band.

He hemmed and hawed for a bit, but when I (politely) pointed out that there had been *several* new singers added to the band in the last month or two that just joined without having to jump through any kind of hoops, and informed him that those new additions to the band had hurt my feelings, he finally hinted strongly that it was likely that I would never be joining that band. He didn't say why (how could he, when he hadn't even said *that* outright?) but he knew why and I knew why. That day, he planted a seed of resentment in me that even now I'm not sure I could uproot even if I tried. That was the beginning of the end of it all.

CHAPTER TEN

I tried to be okay with it, I really did. I tried to move on and forget how bitterly unfair it was that I was still the band's errand girl and had to watch so many others be invited to do the one thing that I so desperately wanted to do from my spot behind a stack of takeout containers, but I just got angrier and angrier.

Not helping matters was the fact that, after that conversation with Andrew, things for me at That Church seemed to just gradually fall apart. John, whom I got along with really well, relocated his family to work at a church hours away. His replacement was a woman who had never really liked me all that much and made me feel constantly judged for one thing or another.

At the same time, a friend of mine in my Bible study group was having some serious relationship drama and had become increasingly unavailable because of it. Meanwhile, the relationship *I* was in was now allowed to be public, and I was so ecstatic about the outward validation of our relationship that I actively chose to ignore all of the very real, very dangerous-to-ignore red flags that had been popping up. But *that*, my friends, is a story worth a blog of its own. My resentment towards Andrew was also starting to come out in my own home with my family which caused some real rifts between them and me.

After that conversation with Andrew, I also started having a harder time being the Good Christian Girl I know everyone at That Church still expected me to be. I got very comfortable calling Andrew out on things. He got to hear about it from me every time he so much as looked at me funny. He wanted me to walk over to Walmart to get some wrapping paper for a stage prop to be used in the Christmas sermon? Sorry, not in my job description. I got to be a real thorn in his side, and I delighted in it.

The truth is that the angrier I got, the more I wanted to make *him* angry. I wanted some kind of payback for all the guilt that overwhelmed me when I was forced to accept that he had tried sexting me and then lied about it. I wanted him to feel even a fraction of the humiliation I felt when I learned that I was the *last* person to be let in on the conversation *about* me. Mostly I wanted to inflict the unfairness on him that I felt he had inflicted on me. The unfairness of losing that stupid internship, even if it was just for a week… The fact that removing *me* was their initial plan disgusted me. The unfairness of the fact that I worked *so* hard for That Church that the paint on the walls was made from my blood, sweat, and tears. I wanted to make him understand it by making him feel it. Right or wrong, I wanted to punish him for what he did that started the whole mess.

Others noticed my rage. John's replacement as my boss in kids' ministry called me in for a special one-on-one meeting. I don't think the *whole* point of the meeting was to talk about the Andrew thing, but it came up. I admitted to her that I was still hurt by the whole thing. Her advice was that Satan *wanted* me to still feel hurt by the whole thing and that I was letting him win by allowing myself to still dwell in it. Besides, she comforted me, their marriage survived it so there was no reason to hold onto that pain. Brook invited me to hang out with her a couple of times as well, where the sentiment she shared was about the same. I tried talking about the whole thing with my Bible study group, leaving out as many identifying details as I could get away with, and the advice I got from the group was that I was hurting myself by not letting it go. If Andrew and Kelly could let it all go, surely, I could do the same.

Andrew and Kelly's marriage was what everyone I spoke to kept pointing me back towards. How wonderful it was that they had worked it out. He could slip into a sinful desire, but they could work through it together. Their marriage was a testimony of God's grace. What did I have to be so angry about? The truth is that I was so angry that I couldn't even put into words *exactly* what I was angry about. What I *could* do was continue to act out, which I did. In abundance. So, I wasn't all *that* surprised when Andrew let me know that my internship was no more, this time for good.

He broke the news to me when I'd arrived for my duties. He asked to speak to me in the church office's waiting area, out in the open. He told me that the church just had to make some budget cuts. Two weeks later, I learned that they'd gotten a new intern. A married woman. Both she and her husband were in the band immediately.

Oh, and I still had to do all of my duties the day that he fired me.

CHAPTER ELEVEN

After I lost the internship for good, I started to slowly fade out of church life. I left the youth band after the very nice guy who coordinated it hinted that my voice might not be up to par anymore. I never got beyond singing back-up for him, and the night that he decided this, he let me know that another woman (whom I'd grown up with) was joining the band as another backup singer so I wouldn't be getting to sing every week as I had been.

I got a real, grown-up, 9 to 5 job during my last semester of college and, as a result, stepped down from my position in kids' ministry. I offered to stay on as a volunteer, but after a while, I even stopped doing that. I stopped going to Bible study, and only two of my friends from that group ever checked in with me to see if I'd ever go back. I said that I probably wouldn't, and that was that. I do think that those two are good people though, and we are warm to each other on social media and when we run into each other on occasion.

Eventually, after I moved out of my parents' house and into my own, I stopped going to church altogether. It was too hard. It hurt too much. It felt exhausting having to go there and put on the Good Christian Girl happy face that never hints that anything is wrong, that never so much as whispers that she might need some help. I was exhausted by the few people from That Church who *did* know about what had happened acting like it was illogical of me to still be hurt by everything and encouraging me to fake it until I made it. I needed to be understood, I needed someone to care about what happened to me, and not to be encouraged to grin and bear it. I *certainly* did not need someone to throw one of That Church's endless supply of feel-good logos at me like a band-aid.

In the entire time I spent fading out of That Church, not one single person whom I had spent years volunteering for, bowing down to, running myself ragged to please, ever asked me if I was okay. I very much wasn't. On the contrary, almost everyone I had once considered my friend there seemed to prefer to ignore that I even existed, or chalk it up to the idea that the problem was just me.

Brook spoke to me a couple of times after my fading, but only to try and convince me to focus on my gratitude for Andrew and Kelly's restored marriage. After that, we've been polite on the rare occasion when we run into each other, and that's about it.

J.T. said hi to me at the chiropractor's office once, and I thought to myself: *there goes the fakest unremarkable man I've ever met.*

A girl from my Bible study group, and I got pregnant right around the same time and happened to go to the same OBGYN. I was reading in the waiting room when I felt someone staring at me. I looked up to see her across the waiting room scowling at me before quickly turning her head to face the wall. That's how the most extreme members of That Church react when you no longer want to be one of them.

Years have passed since this whole ordeal, and I'd like to say that I'm over it, but I'm not. To write a tell-all, it kind of goes without saying that I'm not over it. Far from it, actually. There *are* things that I have learned and things that have happened as an indirect result of my experience that I'm grateful for, though.

For one thing, shortly after leaving That Church, I also found the strength to leave the toxic relationship I was in. It was then that I met and started dating my now-husband who encourages me to be upfront and outspoken in every way, something that I highly doubt I would have found if I'd stuck it out and waited for any boy from That Church to notice me. We have an amazing daughter whom I will do anything to protect from people like the ones at That Church.

I'm grateful for the fact that now I can say I'm a little bit better at recognizing predatory and downright evil behavior.

I'm grateful for the fact that, in a world full of Andrews and J.T.s, the world also still has at least a few Aarons—people whom I believe will genuinely try to do the *right* thing. That, at least, gives me hope.

I'm grateful to have gained some perspective on people. Once, not long after my husband and I started dating, we saw Kelly—Andrew's wife—at the grocery store. She and my husband knew one another in high school. She cut her eyes at me so hard that I could have dropped dead right then and there before smiling warmly at my husband and saying a loud, drawn-out "*Hiiiiiii!*". It bothered me, but I can't say that I didn't get it. It's much easier for her to hate me than the husband she chose to stay with, so I guess I'll have to hate him for the two of us.

Kidding.

Kind of.

I'm grateful that, despite all the bullshit, I had God through it all. None of what happened was His fault. I still pray all the time; I ask him questions and thank Him for the good things I have. I still love God, but I can't see myself ever going to a Sunday sermon anytime soon, and I will most certainly never go to That Church ever again.

I know that there are a lot of people who knew me back then that assume I'm some anti-God heathen now, and that's simply not the case. I don't even consider myself anti-church really. I'm just someone who got to know a little too well that when they say no perfect people are allowed in their building, they, allow a lot of really shitty people to do shitty things repeatedly while using that very sentiment as a safety net. *Well sure, I did cheat on my wife with two separate women, but hey—nobody's perfect. We all fall short!* I hope they're very proud of the culture they've perpetuated.

A couple of months ago, I went on a solo trip to the grocery store. On the way home, just on a whim, I opened up Spotify to start playing "Like A Lion" by Newsboys. I hadn't listened to that song in years, probably since the last time I sang it myself in kids' ministry. I didn't make it more than two rows over from where I'd originally parked before I had to park again because I was crying too hard to drive safely. A song that used to fill me with so much joy now fills me with so much sadness and loss that I can't even get through the first chorus. I hope that one day that won't be the case. I think that now, after all this time, I might be making some progress towards that end.

Afterward

So here I am at age 29. I originally shared my story as a blog and it gained a fair amount of traction, particularly with people who *had* gone to That Church and no longer do. People I hadn't spoken to in years were suddenly reaching out to me to tell me they were sorry, to share experiences with That Church that had hurt *them*, to update me on the last straw for them that led to their departure from That Church, to tell me that they always knew "Andrew" was no good, and so on. That was something I never could have anticipated. Quite the opposite.

When I first decided to share my story, I saw it as a way to purge my soul of a sort of cancer that had been festering in it—to finally rid myself of something that has haunted me for years and something that has sapped so much joy from my life. I bared my cancerous soul for all the world to see (well, all *my* world, I guess), and in all honesty, I expected some pretty ugly backlash from the

Powers That Be in That Church. I expected the full wrath of Andrew and J.T. and the two pastors who founded the place. I expected to be called a liar, to be gaslighted by them, or to be given a halfhearted olive branch in an attempt to stop me from posting anymore. Every evening, when I hit "publish" on a new blog entry, I would have to lay under a weighted blanket just to be able to fall asleep because my heart would be drumming so loud that it could wake the neighbors. I would have dreams taking me back through the whole experience all over again, and during the day, I would have flashbacks to the now somewhat infamous night of the great Snapchat scandal. It was like having to relive all of it, which I guess makes some kind of sense, only now I had the added anxiety and uncertainty of how it would be received and responded to.

The response started pretty soon after I started sharing my story. Friends of my husband started adding me as a friend on Facebook or coming up to me at work to let me know that they were *hooked* and hungry for more. They complimented my writing, which was a wonderful surprise—I hadn't done any significant writing since before the whole incident and it was nice to hear that I hadn't lost whatever magical touch I thought I'd once had. Then came the other former members, volunteers, and even a former employee or two from That Church.

Messages on Facebook and Instagram, and text messages were sent to me voicing support and validation; several people (nearly all of them women) shared with me ways that That Church failed them too. It was nice to have people to commiserate with who got it, on multiple levels.

A former pastor whose child goes to the same daycare as mine stopped me in the parking lot one day to tell me he was proud of me for sharing my story. That one was especially validating since he was a pastor I had always had a ton of respect and admiration for—a real "walk the talk" kind of person. I went to my car after drop-off and called my mom to share that one with her, actually, and we both cried happy tears.

A woman I'd graduated high school with, who also happens to be an ex-girlfriend of Andrew, messaged me on Facebook to validate my experience as well, and my favorite part of that conversation was that we laughed together about my particularly vivid description of the "Jesus weave" and how awful it looked. Since then, she has been a nice person to have in my corner who cheers me on when I have a rare but welcome surge of self-confidence and who voices support when that's not so much the case.

Most surprising of all was when Aaron reached out to me, again via Facebook message. He shared with me that he hadn't been attending That Church for a while himself. His marriage to

Brook ended and there had been some rough fallout for him from That Church. I won't go into the details of all of that because frankly, they are not *my* details to divulge. I *will* say that at the end of what turned out to be a pretty lengthy conversation, he extended an invitation to me and my family to have dinner at his new house with his new wife and their blended family. I said we'd be thrilled to do that and he said he'd follow up with me to pick a day. Unfortunately, that didn't end up happening. I figure he probably just got busy and forgot.

When I first decided to turn the blog into a full-blown book, I initially thought that something my story could benefit from was an introductory chapter written by one of the many people who knew me from That Church when all of the mess happened. I wanted it to be someone who understood that all of the negative side effects of the whole ordeal with Andrew and my leaving the church, and just the overall bad taste in my mouth for churches in general nowadays are all a direct result of That Church's failure to minister to me, a young, vulnerable, and an impressionable young woman at the time. I wanted it to be someone who saw firsthand the toxic culture of That Church that prioritized a married man who took advantage of the very clear power imbalance between him and me and never actually had to be held accountable for those actions by anyone who had any real power to hold him accountable. I wanted it to be someone who had also been hurt by That Church but still had hope that things could be okay.

Aaron seemed like the perfect person for the job. Not only did he know me then, but he was also the only one who supported me through the entire thing.

I knew that with how busy he tends to be, and his new life circumstances still being rather fresh, the chances of him agreeing to write an introduction for me were pretty slim. I sent him a message on Facebook, explaining my idea and asking if he would be willing to write a 1,500-word introduction while expressing that there would be absolutely no hard feelings if he couldn't do it, or if he was just uncomfortable doing it. He didn't even owe me an explanation, a simple "no" would be a full sentence.

Initially, Aaron had some concerns. He shared with me that he had recently started going back to That Church and getting involved again. He shared with me that his goal was to show the people of That Church what accountability could look like lovingly. He shared with me that he wanted to "restore relationships" that had been broken during his divorce and all that went with it and that if I had in mind a way that he could write my intro while still being able to achieve that goal, then he was all for it.

I thought to myself, *this is perfect! This is exactly the kind of tone I was going for when sharing my story in the first place!* And with excited, trembling thumbs, I told him my vision for the outcome of turning this story into a book. I said that accountability was my goal, as well as hope that relationships *can* be restored eventually after things like this. I told him, again, that if he wasn't comfortable with that, then it was not a big deal. To my shock, he said he loved my ideas and would get me my intro by the deadline I'd given him, which was three weeks away.

If you've read this book from the beginning, or if you just turned back to the introduction, you'll know where this is going.

The deadline, three weeks after this conversation, came and went. I figured it was the end of the school year and he and his wife have a combined five elementary-aged kids between them, so he probably just got busy, so I waited another few days thinking that he'd keep me posted.

And then he didn't.

Finally, I decided to follow up, just to let him know that if he needed a little more time, it was perfectly fine! No rush. As a bit of a perfectionist myself, I understood needing some more time. I messaged him on Facebook and apologized for not following up sooner, adding that the end of the school year had been a lot more hectic than I had anticipated. I said that if he needed a little more time, just to let me know. I even added a smiley face emoji, for God's sake! I hoped beyond hope that it was just as simple as that—time had gotten away from him and he needed a bit more— but if I'm being completely honest, I knew the truth already.

Aaron wrote back a bit of a diatribe, the gist of which was:

Aaron:

I still think what I said before is true, about there being consequences for people's actions. However, I believe it is best for me to steer clear from this one... I just feel it inside that I need to continue down the path I am on in restoring relationships.

So, since I am who I am, I wrote back a diatribe of my own in the spirit of honesty. The gist of which was:

Me:

I am so happy that you're finding yourself mentally and emotionally able to restore these relationships! I wish I could get to that point without wanting some accountability in addition to restoring my relationships, but I'm just not there... When I reached out to you to write the intro, I really expected you to say no, so I'm not surprised by this decision, just hurt that you felt like you couldn't tell me sooner. More hurt though, because it seems like a terrible missed opportunity to minister... It's sad, but I'll always hold you in high regard as the only person who stood up for me when an entire church staff also missed an opportunity to minister

to me and to others.

    A little passive-aggressive, I'll admit, but it is what it is. In a follow-up message that came hours after I sent that, Aaron explained to me that he did not want to be seen as "endorsing" some of the things in my story, particularly some of the details and the things that came across as personal attacks towards Andrew and That Church. I figured there was no point in continuing the conversation, so I just let him know that he clarified his perspective perfectly and left it at that.

    I wasn't surprised that he'd changed his mind, and even though I *was* hurt that he hadn't had the decency to at least let me know that he had changed his mind, I wasn't even surprised by *that* either. I guess I'm partially to blame for hurting my feelings by expecting a head's up in the first place, especially since the whole "come to have dinner with us!" thing fell through months before this. What sucks is that I fully believe that he had no intentions of letting me know at all that he'd changed his mind, if I hadn't been the one to follow up with him.

    You might expect that I hate him now, for going back to That Church, and for the fact that his desire to get back "in" with the people there is likely the very reason he didn't want to be associated with this book, but I don't hate him. Truth is, I kind of feel sorry for him. When he went through his divorce, it was like he got kicked out of the popular clique. I'm talking about a full-on exile like if it was a high school drama, they replaced him at their lunch table in the cafeteria and *everything.*

Aaron is someone who was deeply ingrained in That Church and by all appearances, he got much of his identity from *being* so deeply ingrained in That Church. Many people do, who go there actually. So, when he got remarried and they started playing nice with him again and invited him back to that proverbial lunch table, it was only natural for him to go back and lap up all of the sweet approval they dripped on him. Without That Church and the sense of community and love that he had gotten from them at one point, he was probably feeling lost and incredibly lonely and would likely do just about anything to make that feeling go away.

I would know.

The thing is though, I have a good life now. I have a husband who loves me in ways I didn't even know were possible and a baby who is our world. I have parents who, while they haven't always known *how* to be there for me, have always done their best to be there for me regardless, even when all of this nonsense took place. I have people in my corner who constantly lift me up and remind me who I am and what I'm capable of.

The need for validation and authentic kindness from anyone at That Church didn't ever stand much of a chance against the people who give validation and authentic kindness to me without having to be asked, and I guess in the end that's why I'm perfectly comfortable with the fact that I'm probably never going to restore the often-conditional relationships I'd had while I was there.

I'm most likely never going to get a genuine apology from any of the key figures who played a part in my exodus from That Church, and that's okay. That Church is just a building full of T-shirts and bumper stickers and other promotional materials that cover the backs and cars of people who are no better than any of the people outside those walls.

It's taken me a good long while, but now that I have purged my soul of its cancer, I feel like I can finally move forward.

References from the Introduction:

Bailey, S. P. (2019, April 29). *Southern Baptist leader encouraged a woman not to report alleged rape to police and told her to forgive assailant, she says.* The Washington Post. https://www.washingtonpost.com/news/acts-of-faith/wp/2018/05/22/southern-baptist-leader-encouraged-a-woman-not-to-report-alleged-rape-to-police-and-told-her-to-forgive-assailant-she-says/.

Maryville University. (2020, September 16). *Me Too: Sexual Harassment Awareness & Prevention.* Maryville Online. https://online.maryville.edu/blog/understanding-the-me-too-movement-a-sexual-harassment-awareness-guide/#:~:text=Me%20Too%20%E2%80%94%20The%20Me%20Too,harassment%20and%20assault%20really%20are.

Shellnutt, K. (2019, May 21). *1 in 10 Young Protestants Have Left a Church Over Abuse.* News & Reporting. https://www.christianitytoday.com/news/2019/may/lifeway-protestant-abuse-survey-young-christians-leave-chur.html.

Siemaszko, C. (2019, February 12). *Southern Baptist Convention: More than 200 ministers, deacons and others have been found guilty of sex abuse, report says.* NBCNews.com.

https://www.nbcnews.com/news/us-news/over-200-baptist-

ministers-deacons-others-found-guilty-sex-abuse-n970276.

Acknowledgements:

I never would have had the guts to turn my story into a blog—let alone an actual published book—without the support of my husband Daniel (who also takes one heck of a cover photo, am I right?). He is my biggest cheerleader and best friend in life, and I frequently marvel at how lucky I am to have him in my life. It was terrifying at first to put pencil to paper, then fingertip to keyboard and share my story with the world, and I absolutely would not have done so if he hadn't encouraged me through the entire process.

As they tend to be, my blog was raw and unpolished. All credit for polishing it up and making it book-worthy goes to my editor, Dr. Phoebe Wallace. She has been an amazing support system through all of my life's major events, and I am eternally grateful for her. I'm also grateful for the kindness and patience of my mentor and friend Tammy Jo Burns, who was always willing to answer my questions and help me through this entire process, as well as my long-time friend Jareth, who has always willing to let me bounce the craziest ideas off of him.

73

To everyone who initially read my blog and gave me validation and kindness as I bared my soul: thank you so much. It has been incredibly humbling to no longer have to carry this experience as a shameful secret. To everyone who spoke with me to share similar stories from That Church and beyond: you are not alone. To anyone who may be carrying the weight of a similar experience who haven't shared their stories with anyone because of fear or shame or any other thing: you are not alone. You do not deserve to carry that burden. I hope you find the support and strength you need to do whatever you need to do to move forward.

To the people who work at, volunteer for, and attend That Church: you *must* be willing to hold one another accountable. You *cannot* let this happen to anyone else. You have *got* to do better, to be better. You are not exempt from consequences just because your slogan makes you feel safe.

To everyone who took the time to read this in its entirety: thank you.

Holley Lunsford

lives in her hometown with her husband, daughter, and three pets. She is a high school English teacher with a passion for all things lit (as in literature). When she isn't writing, Holley spends time pursuing her Master's degree in Library Science so that one day she can spend her days with her first great love: books! She dreams of being a best-selling author, living on ten acres of land so that her husband will let her adopt every animal that makes significant eye contact with her like she currently only wishes she could, and making the world even just a little bit more kind.

Instagram: holley_writes
TikTok: @h_lunsy
Twitter: @HolleyMcLane

www.ingramcontent.com/pod-product-compliance
Lightning Source LLC
LaVergne TN
LVHW021513300325
807261LV00010B/539

* 9 7 9 8 5 1 6 4 0 8 0 1 4 *